Get l

Get Real!

*Relationship Success
is an Inside Job*

Susanne Jorgensen

bookshaker

First Published In Great Britain 2009
www.BookShaker.com

I dedicate this, my first ever book, to my Mother, Else Hendricks, with love and gratitude for her support, encouragement and friendship. Mom, many times you have said that I'm doing what you wished you could have done in your life. I'd like to thank you for passing on to me your passion for learning, zest for life, the important lesson of 'giving back' and for helping me understand the power and the gift of relationships – and never giving up on them!

Contents

Praise

"Success in love, like success in business, depends on a healthy self esteem and huge amounts of self-knowledge. Many rich folks struggle with love, having 'made it' in business and only by working on themselves and their love lives, in the same way they worked on their success, can they expect to get what they want. Susanne's book is a down to earth, practical guide to doing just that and as a single person myself currently, I will be referring to it as often as I refer to my wealth creation books."

Nicola Cairncross, Author & Founder of
The Money Gym, www.TheMoneyGym.com

Acknowledgments

Just one short year ago, this book and my company 'The Singles Gym' were not even the spark of an idea. It was at a one-day seminar in October 2007, I met Nicola Cairncross of The Money Gym (*www.themoneygym.com*) who became my coach and mentor. She helped to change my life and way of thinking.

My dream of starting an online business, incorporating my skills, experience, education and passions, has now become a reality. Thank you, Nicola, for taking me on the most amazing journey and for your continued support.

I'd also like to thank Janet Swift of *SwiftlySorted.com* and *SwiftCopywriting.com* who has had the painstaking job of making this book what it is. As my ideas spill onto the paper, Janet, with her eternal patience and professionalism, has taken the essence of what I want to convey and created a book I can be truly proud of.

Thanks also to Marion Ryan of *ReadySteadyBlog.com* for her technical support in the creation and maintenance of my website and blog. Energetic, creative and professional in every way, she really knows her stuff!

Thank you to my three younger sisters – Loraine, Julianna and Kellie – for being my cheerleaders and believing in me, no matter what I've chosen to do.

Finally, thanks to Eric and Karina, my children, for your continuing love and encouragement. You must have wondered sometimes if this would really happen – well here it is! As I look at you and your relationships, I can see how much wiser you are than I was at your age: it's so lovely to be able to learn from you!

Single? Again?

You can't believe you are single again – and maybe you can't figure out how you got there again either! You feel your confidence has taken a beating. You don't know where to go to meet decent people or maybe you just can't face the dating scene at the moment. You're starting to believe maybe there *is* something wrong with you and that is why you're single!

Maybe you hate being single and you feel lonely. If only you could meet someone who would love you, you'd feel better about yourself and so much more confident.

You want to be independent but you don't want to be alone. You want to find your 'soul mate' but you don't want to be hurt again. You want to share your life with someone special but you're afraid of feeling vulnerable. You want to be in a relationship but you don't want to lose your freedom. You're feeling confused!

Perhaps you've been in and out of so many relationships but know you don't want to spend the rest of your life that way. Or do you tell yourself you've been single for so long because 'all the good ones are taken.'

Maybe you're in an unhappy relationship but don't believe you can survive on your own, or you've come to believe that this is as good as it's ever going to be for you.

You want to have a successful relationship but you keep falling for the 'wrong' kind of person. You just can't seem to attract the 'right' person but can't figure out what you're doing wrong!

You feel like you've been groping in the dark, using trial and error in looking for your ideal partner and it just isn't working!

If you recognise yourself in any of the above, take heart. This book is for you.

We all want to be happy. New research in the field of positive psychology suggests that being in a good relationship is one of the strongest predictors of happiness.

The reality of life, however, is that at some points in our lives we may find ourselves back in the singles scene. Our knee-jerk reaction is often to jump straight into another relationship to dull the pain we are experiencing.

This book is about embracing your single status as an opportunity to take some time out, take a step back and take stock. You may think about what has gone wrong in previous relationships and, more importantly, to start feeling great about who you are and about how to attract love into your life again.

At the end of the day, being a happy successful single is a precursor to a happy and successful relationship. Successful singles are those who know who they are and what they're about. They live successful lives and they are the ones who attract happy relationships.

You may ask, "OK, why yet *another* book on how to attract love?"

What's wrong with the zillion advice books already on the market about how to attract love?

Besides many of them being boring, sexist, unrealistic, misinformed, superficial, full of unhelpful generalisations and not based on solid scientific evidence, there is a secret that the dating industry is hiding from you!

Here's The Secret: The dating and relationship industry is built on the very same premise as the dieting industry. The simple secret behind the multi-million dollar success of the diet industry is that diets don't work. Likewise, most of the relationship advice out there doesn't work either!

You may be shocked by those statements but think about them for a moment. If the current popular trends and ideas about successful dieting and relationships really worked, obesity wouldn't have reached epidemic proportions and there would be *more* successful couples and *fewer* singles! Statistics paint a different picture: divorce is still on the rise and the number of singles in the UK is expected to rise from 12 million today to 16 million in 2011. (*Times Online* 09 March 2008)

Here's the secret as to how the dating and dieting industries really work:

Experts or gurus tell you what will work for you if you follow the 'proven' method of dieting and relationship advice. In fact, these money-making fads work against the laws of nature. Diets work against your natural psychological and biological needs and drives so you end up putting the weight back on plus more. You end up feeling a failure. (As a psychologist, one of my specialties is working with eating disorders. So, believe me, I know what I'm talking about!)

The dating advice doesn't take account of the fact that you are a unique individual. You are advised how to act, what to think and say and, as a result, you end up being less, rather than more, of yourself. Inevitably, you attract someone who fits the image or persona you are trying to project, rather than the true you. Again, you don't meet that special someone who is right for the *real you*.

So what happens when you've tried the latest fad, only to find that you've 'failed'? Like the rejected lover seeking to ease that aching pain deep inside, you are compelled to come back for more.

Both the dieting and relationship industries are raking in millions of dollars, pounds and euros, from something that *doesn't and can never work*.

And here are a few of the gimmicks that both of these industries use to pull you in ... time after time:

You are told that you can have what you want - lose weight or find your ideal partner *quickly and effortlessly*. You're pulled in because, quite frankly, who wants to put in hard work when you're led to believe there's the option of getting what you want *quickly* and *effortlessly?*

You are led to believe that *one size fits all.* The message infers that there's one tried and tested way for every single person. Again, you're pulled in because there's no thinking on your part. All you have to do is just follow the steps and hey presto, you simply *cannot* fail.

When what you tried doesn't work, you feel like a failure – again. You blame yourself and lose a little more confidence. Then, guess what? Yes, you convince yourself that this new diet, this new dating advice really will be the one that works for you because, when it does, you'll have proved to yourself that you are, in fact, OK. Now that you're hooked you're locked into the cycle.

Those are the secrets behind the dieting and dating industries.

So what's different about this book?

Very briefly, I'll share with you 6 very important ways in which this book is different:

1. **No gimmicks!** Gimmicks make you feel good in the short term (they sell), but never bring lasting success – you constantly have to reach for the next gimmick to get the buzz. Advertisers know it and count on this to sell their products! What I'll be sharing with you is real and will make a difference. If you are looking for a 'quick fix', read no further.

2. **None of the 'one size fits all' nonsense.** It might sound good (it appeals and therefore it sells), but a single approach cannot work for every personality type, and in every context. 'Different strokes for different folks' is a more realistic and honest approach. I won't provide you with 'simple formulae' (yes, they would sell) but, instead, I will guide you into your own personal insights and learning. As you work through this book, you will be developing your own individualised "map" for attracting love and finding your ideal partner – a map that will work for you. So if you're still looking for a one size fits all solution, please go no further.

3. **The 'no effort involved' approach is dishonest.** I'm not going to con you into believing that no effort is required. Learning something new or different does take effort. But I'll do all I can to make that effort exciting and fun. A map won't take you to your destination unless you take action – you have to do something, you have to make an effort. Are you looking for your 'soul mate'? Are you looking for 'the person of your dreams.' I don't mean to burst your bubble but without effort, the only place you'll meet the person of your dreams is while you're sleeping. Taking consistent action is the only way to get new learning 'into the muscle.'

4. **No lies about 'quick and instantaneous change'.** Sure, it sells well, and, yes, change can happen in an instant but it just isn't true for most of us. Each of you is on your own personalised journey and your timing is individual. Realistic and lasting change involves effort, as we said earlier, and it also involves your time. I will provide you with practical tools and ideas to help you keep up the momentum of change. Before you realise it, you will find that the small

changes you work on have become your new way of thinking and being.

5. **I won't pretend that I know what is best for you.** People sometimes get hooked on a guru. While that's nicely lucrative for the guru, it doesn't really help you become the expert on you and on your own life. I can help you take a journey during which you will find out for yourself what works best for you. I have my expertise but, at the end of the day, you are the expert on you - and if you don't feel that way right now, don't worry, you will. Prepare for self-discovery.

6. **I won't pretend that my ideas are totally original!** Yes, it would sell if I told you that I, and only I, had the magic formula for attracting love. Honestly though, is any idea really totally 'original'? I've included research from the world of psychology and coaching. I've included ideas and tips from people I admire, books I've read and I share my own story with you, together with the experiences of others.

The assumption I make is that you're a person who wants to attract love into your life and find that 'special' person. Furthermore, you want to live a successful and happy life.

This book is for you if:

- You're tired or fed up with the way your relationships have been going.
- You don't really like where you're life is at.
- You just *know* that something needs to change.
- You're ready to do something different.
- You want to attract love.
- You're open to learning.
- You want to turn your dreams into reality.

By reading this book you'll discover:

- What makes you tick.
- How you have been getting in your own way.
- How to take charge of your thoughts and feelings.
- How to turn your relationship failures into successes.
- Simple yet powerful tools that work for you.

- Learning can be fun.
- The secrets of successful people.

Armed with this understanding, your whole life and relationships will change because **real and lasting change is an inside job**.

By reading this book and doing the 'workouts', you will:

- Know how to get what you want.
- Feel naturally confident.
- Achieve success in your life and relationships.
- Be more of who you are.
- Live more authentically.

The emphasis in this book is about self discovery, as opposed to telling you what you 'should' do. It is experiential in its approach as opposed to being theoretical. It is about encouraging you to take action in order to create habits of success. Above all, it is about having fun.

A Word of Caution

Reading the book is the easy bit. Knowledge will only get you so far. You have to practice what you learn. Only practice will get the new learning 'into the muscle'.

It's about making small steps on a consistent basis. You can visit a gym every day of the week but until you begin exercising, your muscles don't grow or become toned

I've included lots of questions to think about, 'paper and pen exercises' for you to do and tips for practical ideas you can try. I have also included a free workbook for you. The reason I have done this is because I've observed that the most successful people in the world have one thing in common: they write down their goals, ideals, visions and dreams. The free workbook included helps you work through the exercises without making changes to your book. In this way, I hope that you will be more encouraged to really take the time to work through the questions, tips and exercises. *You can find the link to download your free workbook at the end of this book.*

My aim is that you find your own strategies and ideas that fit with who you are. Doing something different is so much more effortless when what you do is aligned with who you are *on the inside.*

If you think about it, to be successful in anything requires that you spend time, money and effort on education, training and support. Your experiences are part of your learning too. The best athletes in the world educate themselves, are constantly training and having coaching lessons and they practice, practice and practice! In terms of my work as a psychologist and coach, my best lessons have come from my hands-on work with clients, not from all the textbooks I read while doing my degrees.

It's not really that different when it comes to attracting love, finding your ideal partner and getting into a happy, fulfilling relationship. It does take time and effort. It can also be fun. Remember how learning and discovering new things was such fun when you were very young. Think about how much children learn in their first few years, mainly because they see the world as an exciting place full of adventure and they love learning. That attitude, unfortunately, gets knocked out of us within a few years, when we learn words like, 'wrong', 'failure' and 'bad'.

I encourage you to be playful with the new concepts and ideas you will come across in this book. Try not to take yourself too seriously and have fun. You'll certainly find learning much easier that way!

So What's The Bottom Line?

The premise behind this book is very simple: It's about using your temporary single status to:

- Create your successful self
- Create your successful life
- Attract your successful relationship

Too often people 'put the horse before the cart'. At some point, most of you have probably felt a bit deflated, lonely or fed up with being single and you think, "If only I was in a relationship". You focus on finding that person who will make you feel good about yourself, who will be the motivation for you to get out of bed each day and who will give your life meaning.

Goodness knows there are enough popular songs out there that romanticises this idea. The problem is that it just doesn't work this way. One only needs to look at the divorce statistics, the people around you or at your own relationship experiences to know this.

My hope for you is that reading this book and working through the exercises may be the beginning of a powerful journey of self discovery and lifelong learning. In that process my wish for you is that, as you become a successful single and as you create a successful life, you'll attract your ideal partner and create your ideal relationship!

It's Never Too Late!

I was in my 30's and had two young children when I decided to start my psychology degree. Added to that, I had a part-time job. My friends told me I was crazy to start another degree that would last six years. So much for the support and encouragement of friends! My clear response was, "You know, six years of my life will go by anyway . . . " True enough, six years did go by and I am pleased that I *didn't* listen to my friends! It was the beginning of a new journey for me. I had no idea where it would take me but, had I not made that decision and taken that first step, I wouldn't be where I am today!

So, I present myself to you as a person who has been on an exciting, life-changing journey. Maybe, I am just a bit further along the road of discovery than you are at this time in your life. I know what taking time out, stepping back and taking stock as a single person has meant to me. I would dearly love for you to join the journey with me. It *really* is never ever too late!

The question you should ask is this: "When I look back in a few years time, do I want to be in the same place I am now? Or, do I want to know that things are different for me?"

Singles Gym Workout #1:
Visiting The Future & Looking Back

For your first workout, I'd like you to take a few minutes, close your eyes and fast-forward your life to, say, two years from now. As you look back from that viewpoint, imagine you are living your ideal life and you are in your ideal relationship. I am interviewing you for The Singles Gym Radio Blog.

Take your time and really try to project yourself *forward looking back*. Really vividly imagine you are living your ideal life and you are in your ideal relationship. I have a few things I would like you to share with my audience. Looking back, two years from today:

1. Describe the ideal life you are now living. For example, what is a typical Tuesday like for you? Be as specific as you can.

2. Describe the ideal relationship you are in. Tell us in detail what it is about this relationship that makes it ideal and tell us how it feels to be in an extraordinary relationship.

3. As you look back, two years from now,

17

please share with my audience how you got to where you are now. What were the steps?

Write your answers down in your workbook.

Do not worry if you found this difficult to do, struggled or found you just couldn't come up with any answers. Just write down *whatever* came up for you. There is no right or wrong answer. There is no good or bad answer. Suspend all judgment and just write.

Congratulations on taking your first step on this exciting, life-changing journey.

"If you want to discover new horizons, you must have the courage to lose sight of the shore."

ANONYMOUS

Looking For Love

Where are you on your journey of finding your ideal partner? How many partners have you left behind on your relationship trail? Do you keep getting into the same kind of relationship? Are you trying to figure out why each relationship starts out great and then seems to end in such disappointment?

Have you bought and read all those "expert" books on how to catch and keep your man or woman, yet find that your relationships keep ending up in the same place?

Have you just come out of a painful relationship and feel you've hit rock bottom and aren't sure where to go from here?

Are you feeling bruised and battered and thinking there is no point in trying because you will only screw up again? Every new option, possibility or new idea may look hopeful for a split second and then the painful memories come crowding in, reminding you that what you desire just isn't possible and that nothing will work for you. How can it? After all, you didn't succeed before, so what's changed?

Negative feelings drain energy. They dampen the spirit and drag you into a vortex where finding an ideal partner and creating and sharing a nurturing relationship seems impossible.

It is a fact that most of us only seek help when something goes horribly wrong or we're bored with the same old patterns. Some hit rock bottom before finally taking action. At this point, we will do almost *anything* to feel happier.

Why are you reading this book? And why now? Do you recognise yourself as you scan the page? If so, welcome!

While rock bottom is a painful place, there is some good news. Once you hit rock bottom, the only way is up!

What You See Is What You Get!

If, at this moment, you are still in a negative or pessimistic state, it is natural to have negative thoughts about self, life and the possibility of ever enjoying a happy relationship. The problem here is that what you believe in will ultimately determine your reality:

- If you have a pessimistic view of relationships, that will be your experience.

- If you don't believe that a happy relationship is possible, then you won't find it.

- If you don't believe you will ever find your ideal partner, then you won't.

If you want a great relationship, you must believe that *it is possible.*

If you want to find your ideal partner, you must believe *you will find him or her.*

> *"Whether you believe you can or you believe you can't, you are right"*
>
> HENRY FORD

Have you noticed how bright the world looks when you feel in a really good mood? The same scenario takes on a very different hue when your mood is low. Your 'inner world' directly impacts upon your perception and experience of your 'outer world'.

Imagine seeing two lovers completely immersed in their personal cocoon of love when you are feeling alone and wounded. Might your thoughts be a little cynical?

Now visualise chancing upon that scenario when you are feeling happy and in love. This time you might smile in enjoyment of their happiness.

Your 'inner world' directly impacts your experience of your 'outer world'. So if you want to change your experience of your 'outer world', you have to make changes in your 'inner world.'

"All change in your outer world begins with a change in your inner world. The Law of Correspondence says that your outer world is a mirror of your inner world . . . This means that as you see yourself and think about yourself in your conscious mind, your perception of your outer world changes and conforms to fit a picture consistent with it."

(BRIAN TRACY. CHANGE YOUR THINKING, CHANGE YOUR LIFE. PAGES 119-120)

Happiness Is...

Remember the days when there were clear rules relating to the roles of men and women, marriage and the composition of families? It wasn't that long ago but how Society has changed and the rules for dating, relationships and marriage have all been challenged in that short time!

Though life is all about change, the one constant is our desire to be happy. Everything we do and wish for is the specific purpose of feeling happy. The car we drive, the clothes we buy, the holidays we take and the places we choose to hang out, are all about making us feel happy.

Research in the growing field of Positive Psychology confirms that the one factor, over all others, that impacts our level of happiness is the strength and number of a person's relationships. Conflict within relationships is one of the surest ways to reduce our personal happiness.

All you need to do is think about a time you were in a bad relationship. Even when your partner wasn't physically present, you ended up thinking about them and all those very powerful, negative emotions associated with that person would rise to the surface. You may even find that you still experience those feelings as you think about that relationship now.

Now think about what is was like when you were in a good relationship. Even when your partner wasn't physically present, you ended up thinking about them with warm, positive feelings and you felt so happy. Even when other parts of your life weren't necessarily perfect, life felt great.

The aim of this book is to help you take charge of your relationship happiness. Taking the following success strategies into your 'muscle' is the key to taking charge of your love life.

Holding this in mind, let's start on 'the inside job', as Tracy calls it.

I am going to share with you the 7 strategies successful people employ on their journey to success. Throughout this book I will be focusing on practical exercises, techniques and strategies gleaned from modelling people who are successful in their lives and relationships.

Each of these 'workouts' is designed to:

- Increase your confidence
- Increase your self-esteem
- Increase your self-belief

As Tracy so succinctly observes:

> *"Success is an inside job. It is a state of mind. It begins with you and is soon reflected in the world around you."*
>
> (BRIAN TRACY. CHANGE YOUR THINKING, CHANGE YOUR LIFE. PAGE 88)

If you really want to attract your ideal partner and change your love life it's crucial that you take each of these strategies, practice them and apply them on a consistent basis. It is the only way to get them into your memory 'muscle'. After a while they will become a natural part of who you are and you will become confident and irresistible. You will become an attraction magnet!

Simply thinking about these strategies won't bring the desired results. Don't just hope you'll find your ideal partner. Don't just hope your love life will change. I invite you to do something about it. The choice to change your love story is yours!

The Singles Gym (supported by this book) is designed to provide strategies to help you take what you've learnt and embed it into the 'muscle'. Your 'mental muscles' grow and become stronger with constant use, just as your physical muscles do when exercised consistently. So do the 'workouts' and feel the benefit!

Success in life and relationships is there for everyone. Yes, even you. So, come on, no excuses.

*"We must become the
change we want to see."*
MAHATMA GANDHI

Turning Your Love Story Inside Out

Although the past cannot be changed, it is *not* a predictor of your future unless, that is, you *believe* it to be. If this is your belief, then you will act in accordance with that thinking and history will certainly repeat itself. Psychologists call this the 'expectancy theory.'

Those same experiences are repeated because the same thoughts, the same beliefs and the same actions are replicated each time.

It is not the past itself that keeps you stuck, but the belief that the past predicts the future that holds you there.

One of my coaches used to say, "Where the attention goes, the energy flows". This is also what the *Law of Attraction* teaches. In other words, what you focus upon is what you receive.

Patterns are a pretty sure sign that you are living out a belief. When you look back at your relationships, do you notice a pattern? Did you:

- Always end up with the same kind of person?

- Find that your relationships usually ended the same way?

If the pattern is a good one, you are living out an enabling belief. If that isn't the case, then you are holding a limiting one. If you predict that things won't work out for you in the future because of past experiences, then your limiting belief will build that outcome into future relationships. The problem lies in your beliefs.

What if Oprah Winfrey, born and raised in a ghetto and now the highest paid woman in America, had believed her past would predict her future?

What if Bill Gates, who dropped out of one of the most prestigious universities in America, believed that unless he graduated from university, he would never become successful?

What if you could draw a curtain on the past and move forward with a clean slate? What difference would that make?

The good news is *you can*. Beliefs are not facts but simply judgments, interpretations and conclusions, usually formed early in life, which can be changed. You can *choose* to take on life-enhancing beliefs, rather than continue to live out limiting ones.

The first step is to recognise those beliefs which are limiting you, holding you back and not serving you in a useful way. Please go to your workbook now and be sure to write down the answers to the following questions:

Singles Gym Workout #2:
Your Future?

What are your beliefs about your future? List at least 5 . . .

1. _____

2. _____

3. _____

4. _____

5. _____

What are your beliefs about your future relationships? List at least 5 . . .

1. _____

2. _____

3. _____

4. _____

5. _____

We will return to this exercise to look at your answers later.

A Myth About Beliefs

"I can't change my beliefs. They feel so *true*!"

Many times I have heard people say they can't change their beliefs simply because what they believe feels so true. In truth, although you may not have realised it, your beliefs have been changing and evolving over time.

Singles Gym Workout #3:
Beliefs Through Time

Identify your beliefs about each of these areas for each of the ages listed and write them down in your workbook You may ask, "What is..?" or, "What is it to be..?" If you haven't yet reached a particular age, make a guess about what your beliefs might be when you reach that age.

	10-20	20-30	30-40	40-50	50+
Ambition					
Beauty					
Health					
Love					
Power					
Wealth					
Security					
Relationships					
Age					
Success					

Now think about and write down your answer to the following questions:

- Which of your beliefs have changed the most?

- How have your beliefs changed over time?

- What has influenced these changes?

You probably weren't aware of how many of your beliefs have in fact changed over time as it is subtle process. The important thing to remember is that if beliefs do change, even if usually out of our awareness. That means they are not fixed. If that is the case, it means we can also consciously choose to change our beliefs when they stop serving us.

But I Can't Change Who I Am!

The other thing that people do is confuse their beliefs with who they are without realising that beliefs are completely separate.

Beliefs *are not facts.* They are the result of *interpretations* and *conclusions* you formed early in life at an unconscious level. From these interpretations, you created 'rules' which you unquestioningly carried into adult life and which become the driving force behind all the beliefs, behaviours, choices and decisions you have ever made.

On a personal note, at a very young age I formulated the 'rule' or belief that, "Men are never there when you need them." I carried forward this belief for many years. When I began analyse it, I asked the question: "Why did I have this belief?"

Well, my mother married several times. I, therefore, experienced men coming into my life for a while and then leaving. My mother's penchant for men in military uniform compounded my belief because these men would have to leave us for a year at a time to fight in the Vietnam War. In addition, when things became difficult, I remember my mother's words, often uttered in despair, "Men are never there when you need them".

Now that I have a better understanding of her background, I can see how she developed this belief. What I didn't realise for a long time, however, was how I took on *her* belief as my own.

It took several relationships and much soul searching to identify why I was attracted to unavailable men (married men or men who weren't interested in me). I also realised why I attached myself to men who were 'emotionally unavailable'. I was merely aligning my life and my partner choices with my deeply-held beliefs. And my belief about men was certainly very limiting. In short, I was getting in my own way.

Singles Gym Workout #4: What Would You Like To Believe?

Have a look at the beliefs you wrote down in the previous exercise. What if you could change your beliefs? What would you like to believe instead?

Replace each of the beliefs you wrote down with beliefs that will serve you better; these beliefs are the ones that will help you find the kind of partner, relationship and life that you desire.

What would you like to believe about your future?

_____

_____

What would you like to believe about men/women?

_____

_____

What would you like to believe about your future relationship?

_____

_____

Write the answers down in your workbook. You may find your answers change as you progress because you will find more clarity about your beliefs.

Beliefs drive behaviours so when beliefs change, so do behaviours. And when behaviours change, the responses from others are different. Guess what? When the responses from others change, so do experiences!

So, to achieve real and lasting change, you have to look at your beliefs.

If you try to change your behaviours without changing the underlying beliefs, it won't be long before those old patterns return.

The dieting industry is a great example of this. I have worked with people who succeed in losing all their excess weight, only to regain it, and more. I have also worked with people who have had stomach stapling only to keep eating the same amount. Unfortunately, now they have to make themselves sick because their stomachs are smaller. Because their attitude (the inside job) hasn't changed, their behaviour around food hasn't changed.

We live our lives aligned with our beliefs. These clients still carried their old beliefs and so whatever hard-earned changes they made could not be sustained.

To change your love story you have to change your beliefs!

Become An Attraction Magnet

You will never meet your soul mate or your ideal partner when you are desperate to meet someone. If you look in the mirror and see an amazing person with lots to offer, people will see you that way too. If you don't like yourself and the person you see in your mirror, why would anyone else?

Confident people are the ones who have all the fun!

You can be confident too – it's just a matter of looking at things differently.

What You Focus On Is What You Get

When the doctor taps you just under the knee and the knee jerks automatically you are responding to a natural reflex which requires no effort at all on your part. In the same way, due to our instinctual 'wiring', remembering bad things is also a 'knee-jerk' reaction. Making an effort to think about and remember what you did right and when things went well doesn't come as naturally to us, does it? Yet, for the following reasons, this is such an important thing to do:

1. Thinking of all your successes will put you in a more resourceful frame of mind. You will then be able to utilise the information and benefit from the exercises contained in this book.

2. It is important to put things into perspective and to recognise your many successes. When faced with new challenges, you will then be able to draw upon past successes.

3. Research has repeatedly shown that the more successes are acknowledged, the more person's self-esteem grows. The more self-esteem and confidence grow, the more able you are to take risks. You will be safe in the knowledge that failure isn't the end of the world. Inevitably, more success is generated. Can you see the upward cycle?

4. It is an established fact that the brain produces chemicals that stimulate parts of the brain when we do something rewarding or pleasurable. As a result, the brain seeks

more stimulation of these 'pleasure centres' and motivates us to seek out more positive experiences. When you think about what you did well the brain's pleasure centre is triggered and you become focused on having more. And, as you know, what we focus upon is what we get!

Start Flexing Your Confidence Muscles!

So, it's important to start exercising some of those 'confidence muscles' that will help you feel good about who you are. Remember, we attract people like ourselves so the more confident and self-sufficient you are and the more you like yourself, the more likely it is you will attract that kind of person!

"The happier you are as a single, the more chance you have of finding the relationship of your dreams."

TRACY COX

Building physical or mental muscle takes consistent effort because it doesn't happen immediately. Sometimes you need support. I have a personal trainer I meet with weekly at my gym. As he takes me through new routines, I know he is there to support me and catch the weights if my muscles are too weak to do that last rep.

So, if you find the following exercise difficult, ask people who know you well to give their views.

I have borrowed some of the ideas from Jack Canfield's book, *"The Success Principles"*. This exercise helps illustrate the imbalance between focusing on what went wrong in life to date and what went well and turned out right.

Please take your time doing this exercise and do not skip over it. This may be a really weak 'muscle' but it's only by pushing yourself that it will ever become stronger!

Singles Gym Workout #5:
Your Achievements

List 100 of your successes and achievements.

Ask yourself the following questions

- What have you achieved – what successes have you had over the past three years? List every achievement, big or small.

- Now add any major achievements you accomplished longer than three years ago.

- What things did you do in spite of feeling frightened or anxious?

- What are some of the things you did even though it was difficult?

- What did you do even though there was a high price to pay?

- What did you manage to achieve even though you thought you would never be able to?

- What do you do that you take for granted but are aware that other people have commented upon?

- What do you do well that others find difficult?

Jack Canfield suggests that you divide your life into three equal parts and list successes you have had for each period.

For example, if you're 30, think of successes a) from birth to 10 yrs, b) 11-20 yrs and c) 21-30 yrs

If you're 45, do the same for a) from birth to 15yrs, b) 16-30yrs and c) 31-45 yrs

In order to find 100 successes you may need to list achievements like learning to ride a bike, getting your first job, passing your driving test, learning to roller skate, etc.

As Jack Canfield writes:

> *"You may even need to write, 'passed first grade, passed second grade. . .'"*
>
> (THE SUCCESS PRINCIPLES, CHAPTER 26
> 'ACKNOWLEDGE YOUR POSITIVE PAST')

It doesn't matter how you get there, just find your 100 successes. As Canfield reminds us, when we define our achievements we set the bar far too high. Guess what? In defining our mistakes and failures, we set the bar too low. Does that resonate with you?

Are you struggling? Isn't it interesting to note how much easier it would have been to list 100 of our failures? And that's a problem. It's hard to build self-belief and confidence when we spend our lives magnifying our faults, weaknesses and mistakes, while discounting our many victories and successes. Don't worry if you find this exercise a bit challenging. You are not alone. Don't give up. Be persistent. It's part of the process of positively turning your life inside out.

The more successes and achievements you can identify, the better you will feel. The better you feel, the more resourceful a state you will be in. When you are in a resourceful state, you can draw on more resources when times are challenging. Likewise, when in a resourceful state, you are able to note and understand what you do well. And then, you can do more. By continually doing this you can consciously raise your self-belief and confidence.

Singles Gym Workout #5:
Your Achievements (continued)

Now choose the three successes of which you are most proud and three others which you think are less important.

1. For each of those successes, close your eyes and step back in time to when you achieved those successes. Remember what you saw, felt and heard. Try to relive that experience. Write down what you remember.

2. Ask yourself the following questions:
    *   What did you do to make this success happen?
    *   What was your role in that situation?
    *   What skills, abilities, strengths and resources did you have?
    *   What were your beliefs?

3. And finally:
    *   What did you learn from doing this exercise?
    *   How do you feel?

Write down your answers – you will want to refer to them later on.

To keep consistently flexing this muscle, over the next two weeks, keep a success diary.

You will find the Success Diary in Appendix 2 on page 43 of the Workbook that accompanies this book. *You'll find the downloadable link at the end of this book.*

At the end of each day, stop and think about what you did well that day, what you accomplished and what successes you had. Most importantly, at the end of each day *write them down.*

Tip: As you recall your daily successes, close your eyes and remember what you saw, felt and heard and any body sensations you notice. In other words, relive those experiences one more time. By doing this you are getting the success experience 'into the muscle.' The brain wants more of what feels good and so your mind becomes focused on creating more success.

When you face new challenges and learning experiences in the future, take a moment to refer back to your success diary. The exercise you have just completed will remind you of your many achievements. You'll be able to give yourself an immediate boost of confidence, just when you need it!

Confident people, who have a healthy sense of who they are and what their life is about, become magnets of attraction!

Changing Relationship Failure Into Success

Having looked at your considerable successes and achievements can you see you have much more to give yourself credit for than you thought? Even though you are now armed with that knowledge, we both know it won't stop you remembering the mistakes along the way. The memories are still lurking in the back of your mind and have a nasty habit of popping up when you least want them to.

Have your last few relationships ended in "disaster"? When you meet someone new and think you might be getting serious, do you immediately default to those negative memories and just "know" this one won't work out either?

You may think it's a shame that I'm asking you to revisit what didn't go so well, especially after the last exercise when you proved to yourself how successful you are. Let's be straight here. The only way to deal with bad experiences is to face them.

When I was a child I believed a creature lurked under my bed which would grab my ankles if I got too close. Under the bed was dark and I certainly wasn't going to look underneath to check if it was there. I just *knew* it was. So, I devised a survival strategy: to get into bed I would take a flying run, taking off halfway between the door and the bed, jumping as high as possible to crash land in the safety of my bed. It was like professional pole vaulting but without the pole! There finally came a point when I was fed up with the athletics every night and I was ready to confront the creature beneath my bed. One night, I mustered all my courage, marched to the bed and grabbed the cover hanging over the side. I yanked it up, dropped to my knees and ferociously stared into the empty darkness. What do you think happened? My fear completely disappeared. It is only when we face our gremlins are we are freed of them.

While I *will* be asking you to think about what hasn't worked for you in relationships, this time I want you to *have a different experience* by thinking about events in a different way than might be usual for you. So, rather than creating a problem, I will show you how to use past mistakes and 'negative' feelings positively so you make them work for you.

Stop Beating Yourself Up!

Have you ever watched a movie being made? I have several actor friends who are always talking about the length of time they spend 'hanging around' because a scene needs to be shot several times before it is considered a 'take'.

I remember, too, how my family moved a lot when I was a child. Whenever we moved my parents would make sure the move was combined with a short holiday, either visiting grandparents or going to an interesting or fun place. Once, on our way to our new home, we decided to visit a studio which filmed westerns and, in particular, my favourite, *The High Chaparral*. I thought it was so cool to be watching the filming of a scene from my favourite television show! The scene we watched involved a guy being thrown out through the shutter doors onto the dirt road outside following a bar room brawl. I really felt for him and I lost count of the number of times the sequence was repeated.

One interesting point I've observed is that actors never consider themselves to be bad actors, regardless of how many times they have to repeat a scene. In other words, it often took many 'takes' for the scene to be successfully shot. In reality, they actually improved with each 'take', also learning from the takes that didn't go well.

Why is it, then, that when you make a mistake you consider yourself as having failed? Almost immediately, that little internal gremlin starts telling you how stupid and utterly useless you are. You throw up your hands in exasperation, all the while thinking, "What's the point anyway?"

Let's take a look at the word mistake. It's made up of 'mis' and 'take'.

Just as in the acting world, in reality there are many '*takes*' in life. A mistake simply means that you didn't get that one 'take' right. And, just like the actor, it simply means making another 'take'. Life is a movie of many takes and, if one doesn't work for you, don't beat yourself up. Instead, try another and another until you find the 'take' that works!

You only 'fail' if you give up. You succeed when you take the learning from that 'mis-take' and apply it as you design the new 'take'.

There Is No Failure, Only Feedback

One of the most valuable reasons to identify what has and hasn't gone well in your life is the opportunity presented to be more aware, to learn and to make changes which will ultimately move you towards your goals.

Paul McKenna, in his book *Change Your Life in 7 Days*, reminds us that failure "is an attitude, not an outcome." McKenna illustrates this point by telling a story about Thomas Edison, the inventor of the electric light. A New York Times reporter as Edison, "How does it feel to have failed seven hundred times?" Edison replied, "I have not failed seven hundred times. I have not failed once. I have succeeded in proving that those seven hundred ways will not work. When I have eliminated all the ways that will not work, I will find the way that will work."

This reply clearly demonstrates the attitude Edison chose about 'failure'.

Success and failure are both valuable forms of feedback. Success is simply feedback about what works. Failure is valuable feedback about what doesn't work. Neither is good nor bad; both involve using the result of an action as a form of learning. There is, therefore, no 'failure', just another form of feedback.

It's what you do with the feedback that counts!

Singles Gym Workout #6:
You Can't Fail

If you knew you couldn't fail . . .

1. What difference would it make?

_____

2. What would you do differently?

_____

3. What choices would you make now?

_____

4. What would you do next?

_____

Get Curious!

Were you one of those who grew up believing that, 'curiosity killed the cat'?

The thing is, curiosity is a natural attitude we possess as children and which most of us have lost by the time we become adults. Yet, this is the most powerful tool when it comes to using our life experiences as a learning process.

Over the next week I would like to challenge you to flex the 'failure is only feedback' muscle. If you would like to this for a longer period, it would be even better. To help you, download as many copies as you need of the 'Failure is only Feedback' Workout on page 17 of the Workbook. *You'll find the downloadable link at the end of this book.*

The most important part of this process is to suspend any judgements about your experiences. Everything you experience then becomes a form of feedback.

Each time you go through this process, you become the expert on what makes you tick and you become the expert on the strategies that work for you and in which context.

You will discover which parts of a strategy you can change at any time to help you achieve what you want in your life and relationships.

Singles Gym Workout #7:
Fail Proofing Yourself

Each time you think you have made an error or a 'mis'-take or believe you have failed at something, I would like you to take the following actions:

1. Don't label or judge what went wrong.

2. Do get curious about what happened. Imagine you were watching this on a film and your job is to figure out what strategy is being employed.

3. To do this, ask yourself and write down the answers to the following questions:
   - What was I doing at the time?
   - What was I thinking at the time?
   - What were my beliefs at the time?
   - What was my mood state at the time?
   - What images was I holding?
   - What inner dialogue was going on?
   - What body sensations was I experiencing at the time?
   - How did I create that?
   - What did I do or not do to create that result?

- What was my part in the response of the other person?
- What do I need to do differently to get what I want?"

4. If you could make the smallest change to the strategy you ran which would make the biggest difference, what would that be? Write down your answer.
5. What are you learning? Write down your thoughts.
6. What difference does the 'no failure, only feedback' approach make for you?

If you knew you couldn't fail, what would you do to change your love story?

It's All About You

If you want to be successful you have to take 100% responsibility for everything you experience in your life. That includes taking responsibility for the quality of your relationships. To do this means giving up complaining, blaming and justifying.

Responsibility frightens people and we seem to live in a society plagued by a 'blame' culture. It's always someone else's fault and so much time seems to be spent pointing the finger at others. I am reminded of this saying: *For every finger you are pointing at someone else, three fingers are pointing back at you.*

Paul McKenna says:

> *"You are not responsible for the hand you have been dealt, but it is always up to you how you play it."*
> (CHANGE YOUR LIFE IN 7 DAYS, PAGE 21)

True, we cannot control everything that happens and, yes, bad things *do* happen to good people. It is not so much what happens to you in life but rather how you react to it that is important. Blaming others may bring a sense of justice but the reality is that it places control and power in the hands of the other party.

Responsibility simply means being 'response - able.' It means having the ability to respond to whatever happens to you in life. Taking 100% responsibility is about taking control. It's about being the author of your own story. Being 'response-able' is taking control of the reins yourself!

The first step towards achieving this is to assume that it is *within your power* to remove any barrier preventing you from having a fulfilling relationship.

One way to do this is to note whenever you are blaming something or someone outside yourself for not getting what you want.

Here are two examples:

Ladies: You tell people that the reason you aren't dating is because no one asks you out.

Gentlemen: You say you aren't dating because women always turn you down.

To bring this under your control – turn these statements around:

Ladies: Now ask yourself this: "What am I doing that makes it difficult for men to ask me out?"

Gentlemen: Now ask yourself this: "What am I doing that makes it difficult for women to accept a date?"

It's time to start thinking about what you can do differently to change your situation. Now that you have more control the possibility of achieving what you want is greatly increased.

Singles Gym Workout #8: Turn It Around

1. Ask yourself this question: "What is stopping me from having the relationship I want now?" Write down your 'gut' response.

2. Now take whatever you wrote down and turn it around (like in the examples above), so that your new statement is about you. Write down your new answer.

Congratulations! You are now saying it's not your fault that you aren't experiencing the great relationship you want but rather that it is within your power to change the block standing between you and your exciting goal.

In the words of motivational speaker, Michael Jeffreys:

"When you say someone or something outside of yourself is preventing you from succeeding, you're giving away your power to that someone or something. You're saying 'you have more control over my life than I do!'"

(INTERVIEW IN PERSONAL SUCCESS MARCH 2007, P18)

Where you end up tomorrow will be the result of the choices you make today.

The second step to taking 100% responsibility is becoming more conscious of what you are *choosing*. If you don't like the way things have turned out you can turn things around by making different choices about your thoughts, beliefs and what you want in your life.

Whether conscious of it or not, you are always choosing. *It's impossible not to choose.* How you arrived at where you are today is the product of all your past choices. You may not have been consciously aware of your choices. Your choices may have been deliberate, about events under your control, or born of fear, despair or anger but, they were all choices.

Take a moment to think about it.

Singles Gym Workout #9:
Your Decision Timeline

1. Select one part of your life – maybe your career.

2. Track-back to the choices you made, consciously or unconsciously, to arrive at where you are now.

3. Draw out your Decision Time Line.
   - Draw a line which will represent a timeline. The start point on the left will represent today and the end point, on the right side, will represent when you found your ideal partner.
   - Now imagine you are standing at the end of the timeline, and you are looking back and sharing with me, the choices you made to find your ideal partner. What are the choices you made?

At birth we are not issued with a manual on how to live, learn, make good choices or have great relationships. We are all pretty much stumbling through life doing the best we can based on what we know at any given time.

It's important to honour the fact that you made the best choices at the time, with the knowledge available to you. As your knowledge and understanding increase, you will make better choices.

The past has passed. All that really matters now is that, from this point forward, you take 100% responsibility and make conscious choices.

Remember, the single advantage is you. Happiness, better relationships and change is not dependent on anything or anyone outside yourself – it begins and ends with you!

As Michael Jeffreys said, *"Taking 100% responsibility for your life is one of the most empowering things you can do for yourself."*

Your Circle of Influence

The key is to be clear about which parts of your life you do have control over or, what Stephen

Covey, in his book, *The 7 Habits of Highly Successful People,* calls your 'circle of influence'. According to Stephen Covey, whatever we face in life, we fall into two categories: 'Circle of Concern' and 'Circle of Influence'.

Covey also says that the first habit of highly effective people is 'being proactive'. Proactive people focus their time, energy and efforts on their Circle of Influence – things which they can do something about. 'Reactive' people, however, focus their time and energy in the 'Circle of Concern' – on things which they have little or no control over. They are easily recognisable. They're the ones who blame and accuse and use 'victim' language.

Over the next few weeks notice where you are spending your time and energy.

Singles Gym Workout #10: Your Response To Problems

On the following chart write down what the challenge, problem or stressor is.

Place a tick in the area of concern you think the issue falls under

Finally write down your response(s).

Challenge, Problem or Stressor	Circles of Concern	Circle of Influence	Response

1. Where are you are spending your time and energy?

2. Is there any connection between where you are spending your time and your reactions?

3. If you want to take more charge of your life, be more successful, what can you do differently?

The Success Formula

Remember what we covered earlier about feedback? Feedback tells you what is and is not working. You either have great relationships or you don't.

In his book, *The Success Principles*, Jack Canfield offers the formula successful people use:

$$E + R = O$$

Event + Response = Outcome

If you are not getting the outcome you want, the solution is simple: change your response.

If you think about it, your responses are the only part of this formula that you have complete control over. You can't change what's out there but by changing your response you can influence your outcome.

Sounds simple doesn't it? Yet how many of us keep doing more of the same when something doesn't work out?

Albert Einstein is credited with the definition of insanity as, *"Doing the same thing and expecting a different outcome."*

If you keep on doing what you've always done, you'll keep getting what you've always had. Change your response and you change the outcome. Keep on changing your responses until you achieve the outcome you seek!

It really is all about YOU! You CAN take charge of your relationship success

Loving In The Present

All we can experience is the present - those moments of time in the here and now. Yesterday is gone and tomorrow hasn't arrived. Focusing on bad experiences from the past or worrying about possible future problems won't change anything!

How you use *today* will make a difference. As you progress through this book you will become clearer about the kind of life, relationship and partner you really want. You will develop your own guide or "compass" which will help you make decisions and choices *today* that will be aligned with where you wish to be tomorrow.

Baggage from the past influences decisions and choices because rules you previously lived by continue to govern your experiences. You may then make decisions based on *fears* you are projecting into the future.

Remember the saying, "Today is the first day of the rest of your life"? It may be clichéd but it is also very true.

Singles Gym Workout #11: Wipe The Slate Clean

Take a moment to ask yourself these questions:

- If I had no past and stood with a clean slate, and today really was the first day of my life, what would I want for me?

- What would I want for my life?

- What decisions would I make?

- What choices would I take?

- What would be the first thing I would do?

- What's stopping me?

Focusing on the 'now' means you have all your energies, skills and resources available to you. Many people find it difficult to 'be present'.

Each week I receive referrals to see individuals who are suffering from severe anxiety because they spend all their time living in the future and worrying about 'what might happen'.

Sadly, I also constantly receive referrals for people who suffer from depression, anger or guilt because they live in the past and ruminate over what should or shouldn't have happened.

Each has their time and place. Sometimes it's useful to look back and learn from the past. Looking forward may help reduce possible risks when embarking upon something new. It's when a disproportionate amount of time is spent on either that you begin to suffer.

If you find you are spending too much time in the future or past, I would encourage you to try the following simple yet effective 'workout'. Repeat it consistently over a period of time until it becomes a new way of being – and enjoy!

Singles Gym Workout #12: Live In The Present

Try living more in the present by doing the following:

1. Download the Daily Habits Chart from the Workbook, appendix 4 - *you'll find the downloadable link at the end of this book.*

2. Decide how often you want to flex this 'muscle' each day – it could be every two hours or four times a day. The important thing is that you are consistent.

- At a chosen time, stop for 5 – 10 minutes and:
- Focus on and notice your breathing.
- Notice what you may be seeing, hearing, smelling and tasting.
- Scan your body from the top of your head to your toes and notice any body sensations.
- Notice your feet on the ground or, if sitting, notice the parts of your body that touch the chair.

As you do this over time your awareness of sensations will increase and your experience will become more intense.

Though a very simple exercise, many clients have found it extremely useful and I hope you do, too.

Another simple exercise is one I found in Michel Neill's book, *Feel Happy Now* (page 47).

Singles Gym Workout #13: Breathe

1. Count 10 breaths from 1 up to 10. You might want to say the words 'in' as you breathe in and 'out' as you exhale. Follow up each word with the number: 'in' (1), 'out' (1); 'in' (2), 'out' (2) . . .

2. If you lost count just start again at 1.

3. When you reach 10, enjoy the moment!

"Guilt, regret, resentment, grievances, sadness, bitterness and all forms of non-forgiveness are caused by too much past and not enough presence."

(ECKHART TOLLE. THE POWER OF NOW. PAGE 51)

True Love isn't driven by the baggage of the past nor is it driven by the unknowns of the future – it grows, thrives and flourishes in moments of the present.

Keep Your Love Muscles Flexible

The One Constant in Life – Change

What is your attitude to change? Love it? Hate it? Most of us are creatures of habit in varying degrees. We have certain routines in our daily lives. We feel more comfortable with what we know and with the predictable. Strangely, sometimes we even prefer to stay with what we know even when our current situation is undesirable or causing pain or distress. (In my e-course, I have included much more about why this is the case.)

Whether we embrace change or not, the fact is that modern life is all about change. The rate of change during the last fifty years has exceeded the rate of change in the thousands of years before.

Companies are constantly restructuring, people are unexpectedly thrust into a new lifestyle as they are laid off and some of the old skills are deemed no longer useful. Technology is changing almost daily and people are more mobile. Having the same job for life is now an exception to the rule.

Successful people know they have to embrace change or they will be sidelined. Equally, they master the art of being flexible; they adapt their approach or response to ensure they achieve the best outcome from a given situation.

A common misconception in our culture is that professional life and personal life are separate. Yet the reality is that a successful relationship requires essentially the same inner resources as a successful career.

When companies don't grow and move with the change that occurs around them, they die. When relationships don't grow with the change that occurs around them, they also perish.

When individuals in an organization don't take on new skills and learning, they get replaced by those who are constantly learning and growing and keeping up with change. When relationships don't change and don't grow, they die.

The problem is that people often don't grow because it has never occurred to them that they are supposed to.

You are not the same person you were as a teenager, or when in your first ever relationship or as you were in your first job. People in relationships change and likewise the circumstances that impact our relationships change. That means that relationships require constant adaptation. When individuals and relationships lose the ability to adapt, they become "stuck" and eventually die.

What often happens in relationships is that when a challenge arises and when the old ways of solving that challenge no longer work, people get stuck in trying the 'more of the same' game. They keep doing the same thing. They try harder to solve the issue when what they really need is to do something different!

Relationships are like plants.
If they aren't growing, they are dying.

Some people only ever engage in what they know or feel they are good at. They may always eat at the same restaurants and order the same food. They only play the sport they know they are good at, never trying anything else. They believe there is only one way to do something. Not only are they limiting their quality of life but they severely limit their ability to deal with unexpected boulders that appear on the road of their lives and relationships. Successful people know that success in life and relationships don't come from living in their comfort zone!

Being able to *choose* which behaviour is most suitable within a given context provides the flexibility necessary to adapt to the twists and turns that are inevitably presented to us in both our lives and relationships.

Paul McKenna says that researchers in the science of cybernetics have found that the most powerful person in any group is the one who is the most flexible:

"The individual who has the most ways of looking at things has the most choices, and hence the greatest possibility of controlling the outcome of any situation."

(CHANGE YOUR LIFE IN 7 DAYS. PAGE 93)

Some people are born with the ability to think, believe and behave flexibly. However, never fear, it is a skill that can be learned by anyone, including you.

So, what are your beliefs about change, about doing something different?

Believing that all change will be painful, difficult or both is a myth. The problem is people make it difficult. See if the following scenario resonates with you:

Ever tried to get rid of a bad habit? First, you try to extinguish the bad habit by thinking about what you are not supposed to do. Then you spend your time trying to work out how to stop doing what you don't want to do. Can you see where you focus of attention is? It is totally on what you don't want rather than what you do. If you believe that achieving change will be difficult or painful, your mind will find a way to honour that belief.

What if change could be simple, painless and fun?

The easiest, simplest and painless way to increase flexibility is to shift your focus to what you do want! Start exercising the opposite 'muscle' – the one you probably aren't using – and flex that muscle consistently for a period of time. The new behaviour eventually becomes the new 'habit'. Try this 'Flexibility Workout'. It's simple and yet very effective.

Singles Gym Workout #14: New Routines

Think of your everyday routines. Write them down. Choose one routine and consciously do it differently:

- You might want to change the order of when you shower and eat breakfast.

- You might change the order of which shoe you put on first.

- You might take another route to work.

- You might ask someone for directions (even if you know the way) if that is something you normally wouldn't do.

- You might go to a movie or go for a meal on your own.

Get creative – play with this! Start with small things and work your way to bigger changes

Widening your comfort zone can be painless. Each day do something that takes you from your comfort zone into your stretch zone. Every time you do this, you expand your comfort zone.

Over time you will become much more comfortable with change and will develop the strategy of flexibility.

Start with the small 'risks' first and gradually challenge yourself with what you see as bigger 'risks'.

Take action daily and build those new habits. Over time, each small change accumulates into large changes in behaviour.

Singles Gym Workout #15: The Big Impact Question

Think about it: What action would have the biggest impact on your life and your love story if you worked at it every day?

Write this down and start doing it – NOW!

Going a step further:

Jack Canfield poses this question:

"What could you achieve if you took on four new habits a year? . . . 5 years from now you'll have 20 new success habits that could bring you all the money you want, the wonderful loving relationships you desire, a healthier, more energized body. . ."

(THE SUCCESS PRINCIPLES. PAGE 249)

Singles Gym Workout #16: New Habits

Think of four new relationship habits you would like to develop over the next year – one new one every 3 months - and write them down:

Habit 1: _____

Habit 2: _____

Habit 3: _____

Habit 4: _____

It really is worthwhile taking the time to include these simple exercises in your daily routine. Changes in your life and relationships will be happening even if you are not immediately aware of them.

What new habits could bring you the loving relationship you desire?

Feel The Fear
& Do It Anyway

Have you ever contemplated doing something new or differently only to be overwhelmed by feeling that it's all so uncomfortable, weird or scary? If so, take heart. This is a perfectly natural reaction to having one's comfort zones challenged.

But how often has fear stopped you achieving what you really want?

How often has fear stopped you from getting into what could have been a great relationship?

How often has feared blocked the way and sabotaged a good relationship?

As a psychologist, I work with people who have become trapped by their fears. Perhaps they are afraid to drive after a motor accident or unable to enter a shop because they remember the panic attack they experienced the last time they went. They may be afraid to use public transport because of an accident involving a bus or train. One client, who was afraid to leave his home, summed up the situation beautifully. He said, "I'm not living, I'm existing".

How many of you may have let fear of being hurt, rejected or let down get in the way of enjoying a happy and fulfilling relationship?

"Fear seems to be epidemic in our society. We fear beginnings, we fear endings. We fear changing; we fear 'staying stuck'. We fear success; we fear failure. We fear living; we fear dying."

SUSAN JEFFERS, FEEL THE FEAR AND DO IT ANYWAY. PAGE 3)

There is no question that, probably, the biggest fear you and I have is of loving and being loved. The reason we don't realise that fear gets in the way of love is because fear often hides itself behind other emotions, such as anger, blame and judgment.

You meet someone. The chemistry is there: the butterfly in your stomach starts every time you think of this person and you can't wait until your next meeting. Then the voice of fear comes automatically gushing in asking these questions:

- "What if he doesn't like me once he gets to know me better?"

- "What if I really fall for this person and then he dumps me."

- "What if he has an affair like my last partner did?"

- "What happens if I lose my freedom?"

Susan Jeffers' assertion is that what underlies fear is the belief you hold: "I can't handle it" or, as my clients often put it, "I can't cope".

So often the fact that we don't take action because we think we can't manage ends with getting stuck in the *"when . . . then"* game. Sadly, some people spend their lives playing this game.

I'm sure you know how it goes: "*When* I feel more confident, *then* I'll go for promotion. *When* the children are older, *then* I'll think about going back to work. *When* I lose weight, *then* I'll start dating.

The reality is, if you knew you could handle anything – even a relationship that didn't work out - then there would be no fear.

The solution is simple. Accept that fear is part of life and not something to be avoided. All you have to do is collect the tools that will help you push through your fears.

Furthermore, Susan Jeffers writes, *"It is my belief that if you are having trouble in your relationship, fear is definitely involved."* (*The Feel The Fear Guide To Lasting Relationships*, Page 24)

Or as David Steele puts it:

"We want to be independent, yet we don't want to be alone. We want to avoid pain, yet we compel ourselves to find someone with whom we can be vulnerable."'

(CONSCIOUS DATING, FINDING THE LOVE OF YOUR LIFE IN TODAY'S WORLD PAGE 28-29)

Unfortunately, where relationships are concerned, fear is a double-edged sword. On the one hand it prevents people beginning relationships but, on the other, it also locks people into unhappy and unhealthy relationships.

When I was 39 years old I had been very unhappy in my marriage for years. I was at the point where I was contemplating whether to stay in the marriage and continue to be unhappy, or come out of the relationship. What made the decision so difficult for me was that I was absolutely terrified.

I had gone from my family home to university and then to my husband's home. I had never lived on my own. I was 19 when we met and now, at 39 and with two children, I was on the brink of making a very scary decision. Not only had I never lived alone, I had never owned a property and had no idea about mortgages, how to get one or whom to contact. There was a whole world about which I knew nothing; I knew there would be so much to learn. Believe me, I felt the fear!

Looking back on those difficult days, I can see how much I've learned and grown. I feel more confident and am doing things I never would have imagined possible.

I've bought, rented out and sold properties since that time, without that fear and trepidation I felt the first time.

I've gone from being employed to having my own business, working less and earning more.

I'm creating several online businesses, something I would never ever have dreamed possible for a non-techie like me.

I've let go of significant relationships and realised I can survive, in fact, thrive.

I have wonderful people coming into both my professional and personal life in the most unexpected ways.

I'm having new and wonderful experiences such as cruising the Caribbean, swimming with dolphins, learning to rock climb and sailing at weekends.

I'm attracting wonderful men into my life – without effort – just by being more of me and feeling great about who I see when I look in the mirror. I have become the chooser!

Each time a fear is conquered, you grow and become more confident. People believe that they can overcome their fears by waiting for this thing called 'confidence' and come to me for coaching or therapy to help them 'find their confidence'. Unfortunately, confidence doesn't happen by talking about it. Rather, it's a process – a process of stepping out of your comfort zones and of pushing past your fears. And each and every time you do this your confidence grows enabling you to take on bigger challenges. Step-by-step your confidence grows.

Not long ago, I faced and really struggled with a decision concerning one of my businesses. My difficulty in making a decision boiled down to fears I held. If I said "yes", I would embark on a path I had never travelled before. On the other hand, if I said "no", I was 'safe. I was about to have a coaching session with my coach, Nicola Cairncross (www.TheMoneyGym.com) and, as I prepared for the webinar, I noticed a question she had on her screen:

"What Would A Brave Person Do?"

It was such a simple question but it made a big impact upon me and I chewed on it for a whole week. Deep down, I knew what the answer was, "A brave woman would say yes!" And I said yes, too.

Don't worry about what you think you ought to do or narrow your answers because of what you believe you're not capable of doing. Asking the question - what would a brave person do - allows you to be objective, distance yourself from the problem and identify the optimum solutions.

I invite you to read the inspiring article, 'What Would A Brave Woman Do', written by Marion Ryan on her blog: http://tinyurl.com/5zhqyx

Is there something in your life that you're afraid of? Perhaps, it's joining a class, club, workshop or course? Are you afraid to try a new sport or hobby or start your own business? Is fear preventing you from applying for your dream job?

As you think about finding your ideal partner, what are your fears? Are you perhaps afraid:

- To go on a date when someone asks you out?
- To try speed dating?
- To try internet dating?
- To ask friends whom they might introduce you to?
- To go to that party on your own?
- Of rejection?
- Of closeness?
- Of losing your independence or 'failing'?

Susan Page reminds us:

"Learning to say 'yes' means not eliminating our fears, but being willing to act in spite of our fears."

(SUSAN PAGE, IF I'M SO WONDERFUL
WHY AM I STILL SINGLE PAGE 168)

Take a moment to think about what you are committed to. Is your real motivation finding your ideal partner and creating a great relationship or protecting yourself from feeling fear?

When you feel your fears rising to the surface, remind yourself of your commitment to finding your ideal partner and ask yourself: "Coming from my new commitment to find my ideal partner and create a fulfilling relationship, what action shall I take now?"

Then ask yourself: "What would I do if I wasn't afraid?"

Then do it! You can take what you want to do and break it down into manageable bite-sized steps. Just start leaning into it. Doing something is better than doing nothing.

The only way to push past fears is to find the tools to help you go out and do the very thing you are fearful of doing!

Fear Stops Us Having Happy Relationships And Keeps Us In Unhappy Relationships

Successful people take action!

They never say *"I can't"*, nor do they ask *"Can I?"* They simply ask: *"How* can I?"

They see their fear as a challenge to finding the tools and resources they need and they see an opportunity to learn new skills and knowledge.

Fear *causes us to protect ourselves*

Love *requires us to become 'safely vulnerable' in the knowledge that we can handle whatever happens.*

Fear *is rigidly holding on in desperation.*

Love *is relaxing and letting love flow.*

Fear *causes us to close our hearts.*

Love *is about opening our hearts.*

Fear *causes us always to put ourselves first.*

Love *is knowing when and how to put our loved one first.*

Fear creates judgment.

Love creates compassion.

Fear creates blame.

Love requires that we take charge of our thoughts and actions and change what doesn't work for us.

Fear creates anger, discord and coldness between the sexes.

Love creates a feeling of harmony, warmth and love.

SUSAN JEFFERS

Singles Gym Workout #17: What Would A Brave Person Do?

Identify one situation that is causing stress and holding you back. Then ask yourself:

- What about this situation is worrying me the most?
- What would I like to change?
- Why have I not made those changes? What am I afraid of?
- What actions would a 'brave person' take?
- How could I take those actions?
- What is holding me back and how can I overcome it?

Singles Gym Workout #18: Dealing With Challenges

Think about your own experiences:

1. What is the scariest thing you've ever done?
   - How did you feel before you did it?
   - What were your thoughts before you did it?
   - What was your worst fear about what would happen?

2. How did it actually turn out?
   - Was the outcome as bad as you anticipated?
   - Did your worst fear actually come true?

Next time you 'feel the fear' when faced with a challenge, review exercises #2, #3 and #4 in this book and do the following . . .

My challenge is:

_____

My worst fear is:

_____

The resources I have are:

_____

The resources I need are:

_____

My next step is:

_____

When I will do it:

_____

Get Real! Relationship Success is an Inside Job

What's Next?

You've read the book and, hopefully, taken time to work through the exercises. What's next? Perhaps the next step is about really getting the new learning into the 'muscle' so that these strategies subconsciously become part of your very being, part of the Successful You!

People often ask how long it takes for new learning or strategies to really be absorbed into the 'muscle'. My research into this question has revealed the following:

- If certain behaviour is repeated thirty times, it becomes a new habit.
- It takes a month, practising several times a day for certain behaviour to become a new habit.
- It takes three months to get a new habit into the 'muscle'

So, which answer is right? I think it's ironic that we look to others to be an expert on ourselves, don't you?

To be honest, I could give you 'scientific' and 'evidenced-based' answers and it might increase my credibility in your eyes. However, I'm not going to do that for the simple reason that I'm not an expert on YOU! You are!

And if you don't think you are, maybe that's an important journey to start taking. You don't need a guru to be the expert on you and I won't pretend to know what works for you. You are unique. You are YOU!

Here's my challenge to you: Think back to your early years. Remember those tick charts your parents may have put up on the wall to tick the box when you did your chores or homework? Or the tick charts on the walls in your classroom where you put a sticker or star when you did something well? The very thought of those charts may cause you to shudder but they are a great way to do two things:

1. Ensure you are practising your 'new habits' on a regular basis.

2. Track how long it takes you to develop new habits.

'School days' are behind you now so there is no need to feel you are being judged. However, you are now enrolled in the School of Life and all learning is for your own benefit and of your choosing.

Choose one strategy at a time that you would like to absorb into your psychological 'muscle'.

Use the Habits Chart to:

- Ensure you practice your chosen new strategy; and

- Record how long it takes before you feel the new strategy has become a part of how you are.

Then move on to the next strategy!

There's just one more thing I'd like to invite you to do before I leave you to build upon your success.

Remember the very first 'workout' in the Introduction? And the responses you gave? It might be very useful for you to repeat that exercise, without referring to your notes, to see how your perceptions and expectations have developed since the beginning of your journey through this book. I think you may be surprised by how your thoughts and feelings have changed as you have discovered how you really are and what's important to you on the 'inside'.

For your convenience, please find the exercise repeated below.

Singles Gym Workout #1 (revisited): Visiting The Future & Looking Back

For your first workout, I'd like you to take a few minutes, close your eyes and fast-forward your life to, say, two years from now. As you look back from that viewpoint, imagine you are living your ideal life and you are in your ideal relationship. I am interviewing you for The Singles Gym Radio Blog.

Take your time and really try to project yourself *forward looking back*. Really vividly imagine you are living your ideal life and you are in your ideal relationship. I have a few things I would like you to share with my audience. Looking back, two years from today:

1. Describe the ideal life you are now living. For example, what is a typical Tuesday like for you? Be as specific as you can.

2. Describe the ideal relationship you are in. Tell us in detail what it is about this relationship that makes it ideal and tell us how it feels to be in an extraordinary relationship.

3. As you look back, two years from now, please share with my audience how you got to where you are now. What were the steps?

Write your answers down in your workbook.

Do not worry if you found this difficult to do, struggled or found you just couldn't come up with any answers. Just write down *whatever* came up for you. There is no right or wrong answer. There is no good or bad answer. Suspend all judgment and just write.

So, having completed this workout again, it's time to read your earlier notes.

- Are they a revelation to you?
- What has changed?
- How does that make you feel?
- Did you experience any 'light bulb moments' of self discovery?

Congratulations for having the courage to recognise the need for change. You are open-minded and brave enough to begin your life-enhancing journey.

I guarantee that the changes you made 'on the inside' will embrace your experiences of life 'on the outside'. You will attract the partner who's just right for you.

Here's to your success in life and love.

Susanne Jorgensen

Susanne Jorgensen is a psychologist, writer and professional coach who helps singles all over the world attract their ideal partner. She is the owner of The Singles Gym (www.TheSinglesGym.com) an online resource for singles wanting to feel great, create successful lives and attract their ideal relationship. Susanne is also building a free online community dedicated to singles and further details are available from The Singles Gym.

Your Free Singles Gym Workbook

To help you get the most out of this book I recommend you download the free accompanying workbook. You can get it here:

http://tinyurl.com/lfhgph

Lightning Source UK Ltd.
Milton Keynes UK
04 November 2009

145775UK00001BA/68/P